Looking

D0663388

LOOKING FOR THE ANSWER

John Benton

EVANGELICAL PRESS

EVANGELICAL PRESS
16/18 High Street, Welwyn, Hertfordshire, AL6 9EQ.
England.

First published 1983
Second edition 1985

ISBN 0 85234 202 0

Bible quotations are from the New International Version,
Hodder & Stoughton, 1979.

Typeset by Beaver ReproGraphics, Watford, Hertfordshire.
Printed in Great Britain by Cox & Wyman, Reading.

Contents

1.
Why believe in God?

Christianity has survived for nearly 2000 years. Perhaps somewhat surprisingly, it continues to grow in popularity. For example, in Africa, south of the Sahara, the church is doubling in size every ten or twelve years. In Rumania, throughout the 1970s, many thousands have come to a personal faith in Jesus Christ. With the death of Chairman Mao and the ensuing change of political climate in China, access to that country has been possible as rarely before. What has been revealed is that the church in that country is stronger than it has ever been. Even in the materialistic West many people are beginning to wonder again whether there *is* something to Christianity after all. So is Christianity true?

Of course, just because so many people believe something does not mean that what they believe is true. They can be sincere, but sincerely wrong. In considering Christianity, then, the question which must be faced is whether or not it has a basis in fact. What is the evidence for it? Is it fact or fable? Do its consequences fit the test of experience? This issue just cannot be side-stepped.

The New Testament is very keen for us to
face that issue. If we read it, we find that its
whole atmosphere is certainly not that of some
double-talking obscurantist cult. Rather it
positively encourages a spirit of open enquiry
into the facts surrounding Jesus. The New
Testament speaks the same language as we do in
this matter of evidence. For example, listen to
what Luke, the writer of the third Gospel
account of the life of Jesus, has to say as he
begins: 'Many have undertaken to draw up an
account of the things that have been fulfilled
among us, just as they were handed down to us
by those who from the first were eyewitnesses
and servants of the word. Therefore, since I
myself have carefully investigated everything
from the beginning, it seemed good also to me
to write an orderly account for you, most
excellent Theophilus, so that you may know the
certainty of the things you have been taught'
(Luke 1:1-4).

Luke wanted his friend Theophilus to know
what he had been taught as a Christian has a
solid foundation in fact. To this end he had
listened to what the original disciples of Jesus
had to say, but also he had engaged in his own
research into the evidence. It has been confirmed
by modern archaeologists that Luke was a very
thorough historian.[1]

Or again, look at the way John, the writer of
the fourth Gospel, begins a letter he writes to
early Christians. John was one of Jesus' original
disciples and so he begins like this: 'That which
was from the beginning, which we have heard;

which we have seen with our eyes, which we have looked at and our hands have touched — this we proclaim' (1 John 1:1).

First-hand knowledge and evidence are put at a high premium by the New Testament. Indeed it seems that Jesus' attitude towards many of his miracles was to say to the crowds watching, 'Look, here is the evidence that my claims are not simply empty words.' It was the evidence of Jesus' miracles which caused many people to begin to think seriously about who Jesus was. One famous religious leader of the day came to investigate, saying to Jesus, 'Rabbi, we know you are a teacher who has come from God. For no one could perform the miraculous signs you are doing if God were not with him' (John 3:2).

Christianity is sure that it has nothing to fear from honest investigation. It encourages you to take a long hard look at all the evidence.

But having said that, there is something else which needs to be said. We must also remember that we are looking at the Christian *faith*. That means that inevitably there must enter an element of trust. That is what faith is about. Christians cannot prove everything they believe, as if it were Pythagoras' theorem. Christianity is not mathematics.

Christian faith is not gullibility. But it is trust based upon evidence. It is rather like a business firm which is thinking of launching a new product. First of all, the firm engages in market research and gathers the evidence of whether or not their product is likely to sell. Then, looking at the available evidence, they have to decide

whether or not to take the risk and launch out.
On the available evidence, the business decides
whether or not to embark on a step of faith. If
the evidence is good, they do. The firm which
never takes such a step of faith, no matter how
good the evidence, gets nowhere fast. The firm
that does its research properly, and in the light
of strong indication launches out, is the only
one that has a chance of making the profit. Just
so, Christianity involves faith, trust, based upon
evidence.

Broadly speaking, Christianity is about God in
Jesus Christ, about man and about the relationship between God and man. Therefore, in these
crucial areas of God and man, we will begin by
asking the question: 'Do the claims of Christianity match up to the available evidence?'

God in Jesus Christ

We all tend to be a little schizophrenic in this
matter of God. One half of us is cynical and finds
it almost impossible to believe; the other half
finds the whole idea that God could be there
mysteriously intriguing.

To begin with, it must be said that the Bible
never attempts a proof of the existence of God
by some kind of philosophical reasoning or
mathematical deduction. There are two very
good reasons for that. The first is that God does
not want the way to himself to be open only to
bright intellectual types. Why should the rest of
us be at a disadvantage? God is not just looking

for intellectuals, but all kinds of people are
equally valuable in his sight. The second reason
why the Bible never attempts a philosophical
proof of God's existence is more difficult to
grasp. It is this. If the God described in the Bible
does exist, he is too big for that kind of proof;
he encompasses too much. The only reason that
we are able to get to grips with geometry proofs
at school is that we are able to stand detached
from the problem we are considering. But if he
is there, we are never able to stand detached
from the God of the Bible. In him we live and
move and have our being (Acts 17:28). We cannot exist, we cannot think, apart from him who
gives us life and supports life continually. To ask
for such a proof of God's existence would be
like saying, 'Prove by deduction the laws of logic,
but without using logic.' It cannot be done. The
idea of proof is tied up with the whole matter of
logic. And, according to the Bible, the idea of
the existence of anything cannot be divorced
from God. So the Bible never takes this route.
Rather, in the Bible God is there as the great
assumption. The opening words of the Bible are
'In the beginning God . . . ' It is then down to us
to look honestly at the evidence to see whether
that profound assumption fits the evidence.

We will briefly consider three crucial state-
ments that Christians make about God.

1. *Christians say that God made the world*
The Christian sees the world in a very different
way from many other people. He sees every star,
every flower, every human being as in a true

sense the handiwork of God. An old hymn puts
the Christian perspective on the world like this:

> Heaven above is softer blue;
> Earth around is sweeter green;
> Something lives in every hue
> Christless eyes have never seen.

Considering this matter of the creation of the
world, I am continually amazed at the people
who say that they do not believe in God, but
who, when looking at creation scientifically,
eventually have to fudge their position. For
example, in the early 70s the BBC screened a
fine series by Jacob Bronowski, entitled *The
Ascent of Man.* The book of that series is now a
million seller. But this is what the agnostic
Bronowski has to say as he is talking about the
development of wheat on earth: 'Yet there is
something even stranger. Now we have a beautiful
ear of wheat, but one which will never spread in
the wind because the ear is too tight to break up.
And if I do break it up, why, then the chaff flies
off and every grain falls exactly where it grew.
Let me remind you that is quite different from
the wild wheats or from the first primitive
hybrid, Emmer. In those primitive forms the ear
is much more open, and if the ear breaks up
then you get quite a different effect — you get
grains which will fly in the wind. The bread
wheats have lost that ability. Suddenly, man and
plant have come together. Man has a wheat that
he lives by, but the wheat also thinks that man
was made for him because only so can it be

propagated. For the bread wheats can only multiply with help; man must harvest the ears and scatter their seeds; and the life of each, man and plant, depends on the other. *It is a true fairy tale of genetics, as if the coming of civilization had been blessed in advance by the spirit of the abbot Gregor Mendel.'*[2]

What Bronowski is saying is that, as he considers the interdependence which exists between man and wheat, it seems as if they were planned for each other, designed for each other. He is saying that, looking at the evidence, it seems as if there is a *mind* behind creation. Christianity says, 'You are quite right, there is. God made the world.'

As a young schoolboy interested in science, one of my early heroes was the astronomer Fred Hoyle. In the summer of 1981 Fred Hoyle and Chandra Wickramasinghe published a very controversial book on the origins of life, *Evolution from Space.*[3] The conclusions of the research they did led them to entitle the last chapter of their book 'Convergence to God'. They have not proved the existence of a mind behind the universe; they do not claim to be Christians. However, they are saying that from their calculations the probability of life starting on its own, simply from inorganic matter plus time plus chance, is so incredibly small (1 in 10 to the power of 40,000) that the idea of a God who has created life just has to be taken seriously. And the Christian says, 'Yes, it should be taken very seriously.'

2. *Christians say that the Bible is God's book*

Do we find any hard evidence of God's finger-
prints on the Bible? Did it really originate from
him? There are many ways in which this matter
can be approached. We could approach it from
the idea of comparative religion. Along these
lines the archaeologist Francis Andersen comments on the religious content of the Old
Testament as follows, speaking about a man in
the Bible called Job: 'Job loved the Lord his
Father and Friend, as no Greek could ever love
even the best of his gods, as no Babylonian,
Canaanite or Egyptian could love any of their
numerous gods . . . It is a fact easily verified by
reading their religious literature that none of
Israel's neighbours had 'Love God' as their first
law. We search in vain for expressions of grateful
delight and joy in God; but in the Old Testament,
especially the Psalms, such sentiments are
abundant.'[4]

From this point of view the Bible seems, then,
to stand away on its own from all other ancient
religious literature. There does indeed seem to
be something special about it. For myself, the
quality of the Bible's ethical teaching is something that has always made a profound impression
upon me, especially the teaching of Christ in the
Sermon on the Mount (Matthew chapters 5-7).

However, probably the most direct evidence
for the special involvement of God with this
book is its spectacular use of prediction. The
Old Testament book of Isaiah is just one of the
many in the Bible which contains specific
predictive prophecy. The book was written

sometime around 700 B.C., and the earliest manuscript in existence is dated around 150 B.C.

One of Isaiah's main themes is that God would send into the world the Messiah to save his people. As Isaiah describes the kind of person the Messiah would be, the kind of life he would live and the kind of death he would die, it is very difficult to imagine that in some way Isaiah had not had a preview of the life of Jesus. Read Isaiah chapter 53 for yourself, and then compare it with the trial, death and burial of Jesus, and see what you think, remembering that Isaiah wrote his book so long before.

Another major note struck by Isaiah is his prediction that, through the coming Messiah, his God would come to be worshipped by people all over the world. As we look around the world today, we see the fulfilment of exactly what Isaiah said. All over the world, there are Christians worshipping Isaiah's God, the same God as the Jews of the Old Testament worshipped. How can it have come about? All the other nations around ancient Israel had their gods, but no one even remembers their names today, let alone worships them. Why is Isaiah's God different? And how was it that Isaiah was able to say in advance exactly what the situation would be through the coming of the Messiah? Isaiah's own explanation is that his God is not just a figment of the imagination, but he is the living and true God who can reveal the future (Isaiah 42:8,9).

3. *Christians say that knowing God is the answer to life*

'Is life worth living?' Men and women have always asked ultimate questions concerning life. These questions seem to have become more acute during the twentieth century. Our science, built upon a philosophy of materialism, tells us that men are just complex machines and modern technology declares that we are not very efficient ones at that. The advert for Fiat cars which explains that they are 'hand-built by robots' may seem amusing, but not to the man who was made redundant when the robot took his job. To the firm the man is of less value than the machine. In such a climate people may well ask, 'What is my life worth?' 'What is the point of life?'

The most profound questions of life, which are usually looked upon as the domain of classical philosophy, are asked by us all at one time or another. 'What is the meaning of life?' 'What is truth?' 'What is love, and does it matter, anyway?' 'What's the point of it all?'

The greatest human minds have struggled with those questions over the centuries of the history of philosophy. However, those philosophers have to confess that they have no answers. Christopher Booker, the first editor of *Private Eye,* sums up the situation like this: 'It was as long ago as 1922 that, at the end of the *Tractatus,* Wittgenstein wrote what is probably the only widely familiar utterance of any modern philosopher — "Of those things of which he cannot speak, a man must remain silent" (in other words, more or less all those questions which older philosophers took as their starting-point). It is only lately that the artists have consciously arrived at the same position, as in Samuel Beckett's statement, "I have nothing to say, and I can only say to what extent I have nothing to say." [5] Life holds out nothing but a meaningless, confusing absurdity. There are no answers, just despair. This is the terrible cul-de-sac in which atheistic philosophy finds itself.

But if the infinite personal God of the Bible is there, we are led to very different conclusions. Our ultimate questions do have very definite and relevant answers. What is my life? Is it just an evolutionary biochemical accident of total insignificance? No. We were brought into the world in the purpose of God. We are made in God's image; we are unspeakably valuable in his sight. We are made for friendship with God: our lives are totally significant!

What is love? Is it just another physico-chemical process which produces a warm sensation inside me? If so, it is no more justifiable than those other physico-chemical processes of envy and violence which also produce 'enjoyable' feelings in some people. No. Love is a reflection of the character of God who made the universe. When we act and care for others out of love, there is a real sense in which our actions are coming close to God. Love is *God*'s pattern for society. Love is none other than the essence of the Maker's instructions!

The God of the Bible makes sense of life. Where we have a situation of all questions and no answers, surely a hypothesis which starts giving real and helpful answers is worth looking into, and should not be dismissed lightly. The great Christian theologian Herman Bavinck summed up the situation like this: 'Man is an enigma whose solution can be found only in God.'[6]

There, from nature, from the Bible, from the ultimate questions we ask ourselves, we have begun to sketch out some of the reasons why the Christian believes in God.

But Christianity is not simply about God: it is about God in Jesus Christ. For the Christian, Jesus himself is the ultimate proof of God. The straight historical evidence about Jesus just cannot be ignored. He is an actual man of history.

There are three main sources of evidence concerning Jesus. Firstly, there are archaeological remains from the middle of the first century, which have revealed the fact that people worshipped a person called Jesus at that time. For example, in Jerusalem in 1945 a coffin was found, dated by the archaeologists between A.D.40 and 50, with an inscription on it which reads, 'Jesus! Let him who rests here arise!'[7].

Secondly, there are pieces of literature from non-Christian and anti-Christian sources which refer to Jesus. For example, the Roman historian Tacitus refers to Jesus' execution at the hands of Pontius Pilate in the reign of the Emperor Tiberius. Again, the Jewish Mishnah (notes of discussions of Jewish Rabbis from the first and second centuries) and the Jewish historian Josephus both make definite reference to Jesus.

Thirdly, of course, there are the accounts of the life of Jesus as recorded in the New Testament itself.

And if we look at the Gospels, what do they show us of Jesus? What was Jesus like? Here is a typical incident from Mark's Gospel. 'Another time he went into the synagogue, and a man with a shrivelled hand was there. Some of them were looking for a reason to accuse Jesus, so they watched him closely to see if he would heal him on the Sabbath. Jesus said to the man with the shrivelled hand, "Stand up in front of everyone." Then Jesus asked them, "Which is lawful on the Sabbath: to do good or to do evil, to save life or to kill?" But they remained silent. He looked around at them in anger and, deeply distressed at their stubborn hearts, said to the man, "Stretch our your hand." He stretched it out, and his hand was completely restored. Then the Pharisees went out and began to plot with the Herodians how they might kill Jesus' (Mark 3:1-6).

Jesus? He was a very controversial figure, unconventional, incredibly shrewd and one who hated hypocritical religion. What was Jesus like? He was a poor man, yet compassionate and giving to the point where he often drove himself to utter exhaustion helping and healing people. Jesus lived a life with which no one could find fault. He always seemed to know exactly what to do at the right time, and yet although people held him in awe, his life was not stuffy or restrictive, but attractive to people. He was a person who made fantastic claims for himself in

a most serious way. For example, he said, 'I am
the light of the world,' 'I am the bread of life,'
'I and the Father are one.' But at the very same
time he shunned fame and public applause; he
hid from it. He was an amazing teacher, a delight
to listen to; people crowded to hear him, and
yet he was totally dogmatic in what he said.
'You have heard it said, . . . but *I* say to you . . .'

What did his disciples make of him? Here is
what three of the original twelve have set on
record as their honest estimate of him.

Simon Peter.   One day, near the town of
Caesarea Philippi, Jesus asked his disciples what
other people thought about him. They replied
the people thought that he was one of the Old
Testament prophets reincarnated. Then Jesus
asked them who they thought he was. Simon
Peter answered, 'You are the Christ, the Son of
the living God' (Matthew 16:16).

John.   The apostle John is the writer of the
fourth Gospel. He wrote his Gospel towards the
end of his life, after he had had many years to
turn over in his mind all he knew about Jesus.
This is how John begins: 'In the beginning was
the Word, and the Word was with God, and the
Word was God . . . The Word became flesh and
lived . . . among us' (John 1:1, 14).

Matthew.   As Matthew wrote his Gospel, he
was considering how he could best describe the
baby born at Bethlehem. He came to this con-
clusion: 'All this took place to fulfil what the

Lord had said through the prophet: "The virgin will be with child and will give birth to a son, and they will call him Immanuel" — which means, "God with us".' Matthew, who is Jesus? He is 'God with us' (Matthew 1:22,23).

This is the honest appraisal of men who spent every single day of their lives with Jesus for three years. If Jesus was pretending to be something he was not, they would most certainly have seen through him. I was at university with somebody for three years in the 1960s. I can remember this certain friend pretending to a group of us that some poem he had written was in fact an unpublished song by Bob Dylan. The pretence lasted less than five minutes before we all saw through it! If an able student finds it impossible to pass his work off as that of a famous singer, how much less could a mere man pass himself off as God! It might be easy to dupe the crowds who are kept at a distance, but not those who live right next to you. People who keep making unfounded claims about themselves can be at best quietly tolerated, but these disciples came to *love* Jesus and were prepared to lay down their lives for him.

What makes all this even more compelling is that these disciples were Jews. Every Jew is brought up to know what they term the 'Shema'. This is a little passage from the book of Deuteronomy which says, 'Hear O Israel, the Lord your God, the Lord is *one*.' The Jew is indoctrinated with the belief that there is only one God. But here was Jesus praying to God in heaven and yet

claiming that he was God, too. The Christian
doctrine of the Trinity is not something that a
Jew could easily come to accept. Yet these
Jewish disciples felt they just had to accept that
Jesus, too, is God. They felt driven to it by the
force of the evidence.

The religious leaders of the day, who hardly
knew Jesus, wanted to kill him for what they
saw as the blasphemy of Jesus claiming to be
God (John 5:18). But those who knew him best,
who were closest to him, came to see that he
was speaking the truth when he said, 'Anyone
who has seen me has seen the Father' (John
14:9).

2.
What has gone wrong with the world?

Christianity is about God entering the world himself in the person of Jesus. But secondly, Christianity is about man. It provides a radical analysis of the essential nature and true problems which confront the human race.

Man

Christianity has a great deal to say about us. Let us consider for a moment whether or not the Christian diagnosis of man's condition rings true. We must widen our horizons to consider not only the evidence about God, but also the evidence about ourselves. What the Bible has to say about man is very blunt and is not very flattering. Often the reason why people do not become Christians is not through lack of evidence about God and about Christ, but because they do not like what Christianity has to say about themselves. People tend to extremes in their consideration of man. There are the blind optimists at one end of the scale, who can look at the world and its troubles and still believe that we will get it all sorted out soon. Utopia is just around the corner; it is just a matter of getting their favourite political party into power. At the other end of the spectrum there are the prophets of doom, who can only view the future with total pessimism. Man is cruel. Who is right?

Christianity says basically two things about mankind.

1. Originally man and woman were made in the image of God

In the first chapter of the Bible we read, 'So God created man in his own image, in the image of God he created him; male and female he created them' (Genesis 1:27). God is the personal, powerful Creator, who speaks to men. God made us in his image, with personality, the power to communicate, the ability to be creative. The fact that we are made in God's image places an incredible dignity upon each human being. There is no such thing as a worthless human life.

We see man's amazing scientific achievements, and occasionally in the news read of acts of self-less heroism in helping fellow men. These things mark men off completely from all other creatures. Christianity says, 'Yes, there is something noble and excellent about man; he is related to God in a unique way, originally created as the image of God.' Then we must go on to see something else as we analyse man.

2. Something has gone terribly wrong with man

We can surely see this fact when we are confronted with statistics like these, which come

from the *New Internationalist Magazine* from
January 1980: 'The money required to provide
adequate food, water, education, health and
housing for everyone in the world has been
estimated at 17 billion dollars a year. It is a huge
sum of money . . . about as much as the world
spends on arms every 2 weeks.'

Something has gone dreadfully wrong with
the world. Probably everyone agrees with that.
But the Christian gospel comes much nearer
home. It declares that it is not just the world
that has gone wrong; it is man himself. It is not
just the system which needs changing; it is the
human heart.

Andrew is someone I know who recently
came to Christ. A young and gifted economist,
he became a Christian after spending much time
doing research into the needs of under-developed
countries. He came to see exactly what needed
to be done. However, what brought him up
short was the fact that, having seen the needs so
exactly, as he looked into his own heart, he
found there no real motivation to go and help
those poor people. He found that although he
knew what was right, the problem was the
selfishness and hardness of his own heart which
stopped him going and getting involved. The
human heart needs to be changed.

Do not misunderstand — Christians are all in
favour of education and social justice, but they
do not see the need for these things as the
ultimate answer to man's problems. Let me
quote a Christian writer, Bruce Milne, who has
summed up the position very well. 'It is this

truth which is the rock upon which all schemes
which attempt to transform the human character
by changing external factors eventually founder.
This is why education without moral transformation will simply produce educated devils
instead of foolish ones. You cannot build a new
society until you have new people. It is this
which is the impasse for Marxism (*and any other
purely political ideology*). Social and economic
relationships are quite simply *not* the ultimate
determinants of character. Thus the revolution
only changes the context in which human selfishness and greed find expression'[8] (italics mine).

There is something perverse, rebellious, bitter,
wayward inside each of us. This is what the
Bible calls 'sin'. This is the problem. If you have
brought up children, you will know, for example,
that it is quite a struggle to get them to say
'please' and 'thank you' as they should. It is
something they seem to have great difficulty in
learning. But no one has to teach them how to
boast or tell a lie: that is something which just
seems to come naturally. It is often such a
struggle to get them to share their toys, but you
do not have to ask twice about what they would
next like to buy from the toyshop. We were the
same when we were children. Man seems cursed
with these things which are 'natural'.

There is often a lot to be learnt by contrasting
opposites. Here is a passage of the Bible which
perhaps more than any other brings the problem
of sin into sharp focus: 'And now I will show
you the most excellent way. If I speak in the
tongues of men and of angels, but have not love,

I am only a resounding gong or a clanging cymbal. If I have the gift of prophecy, and can fathom all mysteries and all knowledge, and if I have a faith that can move mountains but have not love, I am nothing. If I give all I possess to the poor and surrender my body to the flames, but have not love, I gain nothing. Love is patient, love is kind. It does not envy, it does not boast, it is not proud. It is not rude, it is not self-seeking, it is not easily angered, it keeps no record of wrongs. Love does not delight in evil but rejoices with the truth. It always protects, always trusts, always hopes, always perseveres. Love never fails' (1 Corinthians 12:31-13:8).

No one has to prove to us that this is the way we all should be living among our families and friends and workmates. We read this description of love and we all know deep inside us that this is how we should live. We just know it is right, yet we cannot, we will not live like that. That is the crux of what sin is about.

So we can see very often on the TV screen the desperate plight of people in the poorer parts of the Third World, and yet be unmoved and mentally turn our back on it all and happily spend our money on so many things which we do not need. Our sights are set on a bigger house, a bigger car or whatever, when so many people do not have any food, let alone a house and a car.

So the young man can look at a girl and think, 'I'd never want to marry her and give myself to that person in care and selfless love, but I don't mind just using her for the night.' The same thing goes through a girl's mind.

So many people can carry bitter grudges in their hearts against other people. Others honestly do regard themselves as a cut above and more important than other people. Aren't those the facts? This is what sin is all about.

And it all stinks before God. We have our excuses and our so-called extenuating circumstances, and it still stinks. The world is simply a reflection of the state of the human heart — it is in a mess. It is cursed with all the evils for which human nature shows so much potential — war, injustice, pollution, poverty and much more. Jesus said, 'From within, out of men's hearts, come evil thoughts, sexual immorality, theft, murder, adultery, greed, malice, deceit, lewdness, envy, slander, arrogance . . . All these evils come from inside and make a man "unclean"' (Mark 7:20).

Christianity declares that this matter of *sin* has severed the links between God and man. It separates one human being from another, and it also separates humankind from God.

Why does God seem so far away? Why does he never seem to be around when I would like him to be? Why does he seem so hard to find? 'The arm of the Lord is not too short to save, nor his ear too dull to hear. But your iniquities have separated you from your God; your *sins* have hidden his face from you, so that he will not hear' (Isaiah 59:1). If you are to find God, it is the problem of sin which must be dealt with.

Christianity is about God in Jesus Christ, and about man alienated from God. But there is a third matter which belongs so much to the essence of the Christian faith.

God is not the aloof, distant, detached god of Plato or Islam, away somewhere in unconcerned, undisturbed meditation, on the shores of some seventh heaven. God is the God who acts, who loves, who intervenes. God is a God who is desperately concerned and anxious about man's situation. So it is that God has stepped into history in the person of his Son, Jesus, and the result was a cross. The cross has so much to tell us about the true message of Christianity.

The cross

'Pilate tried to set Jesus free, but the Jews kept shouting, "If you let this man go, you are no friend of Caesar. Anyone who claims to be a king opposes Caesar." When Pilate heard this, he brought Jesus out and sat down on the judge's seat at a place known as The Stone Pavement (which in Aramaic is Gabbatha). It was the day of Preparation of Passover Week, about the sixth hour. "Here is your king." Pilate said to the Jews. But they shouted, "Take him away! Take him away! Crucify him!" "Shall I crucify your king?" Pilate asked. "We have no king but Caesar," the chief priests answered. Finally Pilate handed him over to them to be crucified. So the soldiers took charge of Jesus. Carrying his own cross, he went out to The Place of the Skull (which in Aramaic is called Golgotha). Here they crucified him, and with him two others — one

on each side and Jesus in the middle' (John
19:12-19).

The cross provides us with the ultimate
evidence concerning the nature of the human
heart. Man is capable of incredible evil because
he is alienated from God. To those who say,
'Well, surely the human race isn't all that bad?'
Christianity points to the cross. The greatest
proof that man is thoroughly alienated from
God is the way man treated God when he came
in the person of Jesus. We crucified him.

But besides being the great indicator of the
real temperature of man's rebellion against God,
the cross also records for us the fervency of
God's love for man. While God did not instigate
man's hatred of Jesus, the cross was in his plan
to deal with man's sin so that he could be forgiven and reconciled to God. Man is guilty with
sin, man is sick with sin, but the cross deals with
all that. The actions of pitiless men against God
are turned into blessing to man by God. This is
the wonderful God that he is. Cruelty is turned
into kindness at the cross.

Man is both guilty before God because of his
sin, and sick spiritually with sin, in that he is cut
off from God, the source of real life. He is guilty
and he is sick. Let us see how the cross is the
answer to sin.

God prepared the way for our understanding
of the cross by setting it up in the particular
context of the nation he had specially prepared,
the Jews. The Old Testament ceremonies and
the history of the Jewish people provided the
background information which enables us to

interpret what Jesus did on the cross. This whole matter of understanding the cross is a large study in itself, but we will just note two simple pictures which are used to explain what Jesus did in dying on the cross.

1. *The lamb*

The picture of a lamb shows us particularly how Jesus deals with our guilt because of sin before God. Our guilt before God is a terrible reality. Many people feel it in their own consciences. I can remember, once when I was in Wales, getting into conversation with a young man I had never met before. His feeling of guilt and distress was such that he felt he had to talk to somebody. His girl-friend had become pregnant; they had decided to have the child, but the mother had died in childbirth. Here was this poor fellow, heart-broken and with terrible pangs of conscience over the whole dreadful situation. One could not help but feel for him. But we need to realize that human guilt is not simply self-accusation. For us all it indicates something of our guilt before God.

How does the cross of Jesus deal with our guilt? John the Baptist was sent by God to the Jews as the one who was to prepare the way and introduce Jesus to the nation. When John the Baptist saw Jesus, he shouted to everyone watching that day, 'Look, the Lamb of God, who takes away the sin of the world!' (John 1:29.) What did he mean?

In the Old Testament religious ceremonies of the Jews, when a man was guilty of wrongdoing and sin, he would come to the special tent of God with an animal, a lamb. Then before God he would place his hands upon the animal's head and confess his sins, own up to what he had done wrong, and this symbolized the transference of the man's guilt to the animal. The animal was killed as punishment for the man's sin. The animal was killed as a substitute for the man who was sorry for his sin.

The Christian gospel is that, although sin carries the death penalty, Jesus was the substitute sin-bearer for everyone who puts their trust in him. Just as the hands laid on the head of the animal joined the person to the animal and the guilt was transferred, just so faith in Jesus joins people to him, so that our guilt becomes his. The guilt of sin has been laid on him and he paid the death penalty, the physical and spiritual death penalty, for everyone who has faith in him.

The apostle Paul describes how Jesus takes away our guilt and makes us right with God: "God made him who had no sin to be sin for us, so that in him we might become the righteousness of God" (2 Corinthians 5:21).

2. *The snake*
Another aspect of the work of Christ on the cross is conveyed to us in the unlikely picture of a snake. The picture of a snake refers particularly to the fact that Jesus is able to cure the spiritual sickness of man's sin.

Sin is like a poison which is ruining human society, bringing loneliness, cruelty, fear and frustration. This sickness causes man to die eternally because it separates us from God. Jesus himself took up an Old Testament story which points to how he is able by his cross to deal with the sickness of sin in our lives. At the time when Moses was leading the Israelites, their camp was invaded by poisonous snakes. Everyone who was bitten by the snakes was dead or dying. Moses asked God what to do, and God told him to make a replica of a snake out of brass and put it up on a pole in the middle of the Israelite camp. When any of the people were bitten, if they looked towards the snake on the pole, they would live. Jesus said about himself being lifted up on the cross, 'Just as Moses lifted up the snake in the desert, so the Son of Man must be lifted up, that everyone who believes may have eternal life' (John 3:14,15).

The snake was God's instrument to which the Israelites looked for physical healing. Jesus is the one to whom we must look in faith for spiritual healing. Our lives can be transformed, our lives can be changed radically from sin as we look to Jesus. As a person looks at what Jesus did for him on the cross, and realizes how much Jesus loved him, he begins to be transformed, to stop living for self, and to live for the one who loved him so much as to die for him. The cross brings a spiritual transformation. It brings spiritual healing, putting us back in touch with God, as our guilt is taken away and our hearts are changed from being alienated from God to loving him for what he has done.

The prophet Isaiah brings together these two aspects — the removal of guilt through Christ paying the penalty, and the healing from the spiritual sickness of sin — as he foretells the suffering of Jesus: 'But he was pierced for our transgressions, he was crushed for our iniquities; the punishment that brought us peace was upon him, and by his wounds we are healed' (Isaiah 53:5).

We are not put right with God by trying to do better. Nor do we overcome sin by becoming moralists. People are put right with God by what Jesus did on the cross as they put their faith in him.

3.
Is there an answer to suffering?

It is evening in the hospital. The doctor has handed in his 'bleep' so that he will not be disturbed. After a few words with the sister he enters the small ward. It is the first time the patient has seen him in his ordinary clothes without his white coat. The doctor pulls one of the separating curtains and sits on the patient's bed. For the first time all formality is gone. The doctor's quiet voice whispers, 'The biopsy shows that the cancer cells are still there. I'm afraid there is nothing we can do . . . ' And the patient bursts into tears.

While I was a teacher on Merseyside there was a boy in the school whose father died. I think the father knew that he had terminal cancer and in the last days the family went away on holiday to be together. While they were there the father died. The young boy was extremely upset by the loss of his father, as they had been very close. For some time after the father's death the boy would stay in his bedroom each evening and listen to his father's voice on the cassette recorder, over and over again, trying to bring back the past. Death is the final heart-break, total separation.

Viewing cases like these, we feel constrained
to ask, 'Is that the end?' 'Is there life after
death?'

But this matter of death really leads into the
whole matter of human suffering. Death is
simply the climax, the pinnacle of the whole
mountain.

I have an African friend who ministers Christ's
gospel in one of the poorest parts of Kenya. The
problems of poverty and malnutrition are just
terrible. One summer fifteen children were lost
to diseases which, had the children been properly
fed, they could have coped with easily. Yet, of
course, what goes on in Josiah's small community
is only a small sample of the situation world-
wide.

Perhaps non-religious people find it most easy
to identify with the cross of Jesus as a symbol of
human suffering. For many people the image of
suffering is the image which understandably
dominates the view they have of the world,
whether it is natural disasters or the inhumanity
of man to his fellow man.

The French playwright Eugene Ionesco writes
like this about the way violence has profoundly
affected his outlook as a person: 'Shortly after
my arrival in my second homeland, I saw a man,
still young, big and strong, attack an old man
with his fists and kick him with his boots . . . I
have no other images of the world except those
of evanescence and brutality, vanity and rage,
nothingness or hideousness, useless hatred.
Everything I have experienced has merely
confirmed what I had seen and understood in

my childhood: vain and sordid fury, cries suddenly stifled by silence, shadows engulfed forever in the night.'⁹

There is injustice and suffering, and all the world has to say to us is something like, 'Grin and bear it,' or, 'Get involved in terrorism to change the system' (as if more killing will lead to less misery), or, 'Drown your sorrows in a bottle of whatever and forget about it.' At that point we throw up our hands in despair. We ask, 'Why is there so much suffering and how can we live with it?' Many people are kept from becoming Christians simply because they have honest difficulties over the heart-breaking subject of human suffering. 'Doesn't God care?' 'What is the answer?'

We all face painful crises in our lives. We must all face the final crisis of death. 'Does the Christian faith have anything positive to say, anything relevant and definite to offer people concerning suffering?' That is a fair question. The first thing that Christianity has to say about death and suffering is that their presence in the world is a direct consequence of man's alienation from God.

God is the ultimate source of all life and well-being. If man has rejected God, if man has pulled the plug on the power supply, then inevitably his world is thrown out of harmony with itself, inevitably the consequence is death. Jesus said that the great commandment is 'Love the Lord your God with all your heart.' But man replies, 'No, we don't want God.'

We should love our neighbours and care for

them in the same way we love and care for ourselves. Our individual rejection of this, God's
other great commandment, only serves to make
the situation worse. Leaving people in poverty
does make the temptation to stealing and crime
greater. It does not excuse the poor criminal,
but it does put pressures upon him which are
not on others.

The selfishness of some leads to the selfishness
of others. We begin to see something of the
terrible element of God's judgement in that God
gives people up to follow their own ways. The
complex web of sin encourages human beings to
strangle each other in suffering.

The Christian gospel has, however, something
very positive to say to us as well on these matters
of suffering and death. The key to it all is the
resurrection of Jesus. If Jesus is alive from the
dead, it has the most profound implications.

If Jesus did rise from death, it calls into
question all the assumptions which underlie the
materialistic world-view of our society. At school
we are taught materialism. No, we do not have
any lessons in it, but it is taught in every class.
We are taught from an early age that the only
things which matter, the only things which exist,
are the things you can taste, touch, smell, hear
and see. Death is the end, and therefore we must
adopt the philosophy of 'Eat, drink and be merry
for tomorrow we die'. So we are brainwashed
into believing that success in life means business
success, academic success, sporting success. The
question as to whether a person is loving, patient,
kind and loyal is viewed as largely irrelevant.

'How much does he earn?' 'What grades did he get?' These are the questions our society operates on, and that sort of attitude is producing a hard, lonely and cutthroat world. We used to have a careers convention at the school where I worked, where boys could meet people from the various professions they were considering going in for. I can vividly remember that while the chartered accountant's room was packed to the doors, the people involved in community care saw two boys all day. From a materialistic world-view, community care does not come out too well: your patience might be tried and the pay is not very good (until you get into the management side, of course!)

But suppose this life is not all. Suppose Jesus did survive death. Suppose we will all have to give an account to God as to how we have lived and how we have treated our fellow men. Suppose there is a heaven and a hell. Suppose there is life after death. If it is true, the resurrection of Jesus has the most sweeping implications for our system of values and the way we live our lives.

The resurrection

'Early on the first day of the week, while it was still dark, Mary of Magdala went to the tomb and saw that the stone had been removed from the entrance. So she came running to Simon Peter and the other disciple, the one Jesus loved, and said, "They have taken the Lord out of the tomb, and we don't know where they have put him!"

'So Peter and the other disciple started for the tomb. Both were running, but the other disciple outran Peter and reached the tomb first. He bent over and looked in at the strips of linen lying there but did not go in. Then Simon Peter, who was behind him, arrived and went into the tomb. He saw the strips of linen lying there, as well as the burial cloth that had been around Jesus' head. The cloth was folded up by itself, separate from the linen. Finally the other disciple, who had reached the tomb first, also went inside. He saw and believed. (They still did not understand from Scripture that Jesus had to rise from the dead)' (John 20:1-9).

What did happen that Sunday morning in Jerusalem after Jesus had been crucified? How did the early church come to believe that he was alive from the dead?

1. Did the disciples steal the body? That was one of the first accusations made against the Christians. The Jewish authorities had asked the Romans to place a guard of soldiers at the tomb to prevent that very thing (Matthew 27:62-66).

But, 'While the women were on their way, some of the guards went into the city and reported to the chief priests everything that had happened. When the chief priests had met with the elders and devised a plan, they gave the soldiers a large sum of money, telling them, "You are to say, 'His disciples came during the night and stole him away while we were asleep.' If this report gets to the governor, we will satisfy him and keep you out of trouble." So the soldiers took the money and did as they were instructed. And this story has been widely circulated among the Jews to this very day' (Matthew 28:11-15).

Is it reasonable that a bunch of men who had fled when Jesus had been arrested should go to a tomb guarded by Roman soldiers, trained and skilled in war, and overcome them? Is it reasonable that, having done this, they would then risk their lives, and even lay down their lives, for going about preaching that 'Jesus is alive'? Is it feasible that the Christian message could have been believed and spread so quickly with this kind of false foundation? Wouldn't at least one of those grave-robbers, on his deathbed, have let the cat out of the bag?

2. Did the authorities remove the body for some devious reason? Well, the disciples of Jesus later caused enough trouble to the authorities by their preaching. If this was the case, why didn't the authorities just produce the corpse and silence the whole thing?

3. Were the disciples mistaken about which tomb Jesus had been buried in? But would they all have gone separately to the wrong tomb? And, anyway, wouldn't the authorities soon have put them right to shut them up?

4. Perhaps persons unknown stole the body of Jesus and so duped both the disciples and the Jewish and Roman authorities? Was the body of Jesus lost? The real trouble with that argument,

and in fact all the explanations we have listed so
far, is that the disciples did not preach about an
empty tomb. The disciples preached that they
had *seen Jesus* alive.

'For what I received I passed on to you as of
first importance: that Christ died for our sins
according to the Scriptures, that he was buried,
that he was raised on the third day according to
the Scriptures, and that he appeared to Peter,
and then to the Twelve. After that, he appeared
to more than five hundred of the brothers at the
same time, most of whom are still living, though
some have fallen asleep. Then he appeared to
James, then to all the apostles, and last of all
he appeared to me also, as to one abnormally
born' (1 Corinthians 15:3-8).

They preached that they had met Jesus alive
from the dead.

5. Perhaps their seeing Jesus was just a halluci-
nation? But hallucinations occur only to indi-
viduals. This is because they originate in the
subconscious mind of the person. So no two
persons would see the same thing. But here many
people saw him at the same time. Jewish people,
from their law, would not accept any evidence,
anyway, unless it came from two or three
witnesses at least.

The Christian church suddenly exploded upon
the history of the world with irrepressible force!
Depressed and despairing after Jesus had been
put to death, the disciples were suddenly transformed into people who preached fearlessly, joy-
fully and with great ebullience that there is life

after death and that heaven is open to all who
will trust in Jesus. The proof of it all, they said,
was that they had met Jesus after he had con-
quered death. They were unafraid of civil authorities, they were unafraid of death, they changed
the world with their message. All these things
defy explanation, unless, of course, as they
claimed, Jesus really did rise.

The apostle Paul was a man who was such a
sceptic, and so sure that this Christianity was
nonsense and that Jesus was dead that he began
to persecute the church. Yet he was converted
to Christianity when, according to his own story,
he met the risen Lord Jesus Christ on the way to
Damascus.

There have been two other famous attempts
by sceptics to knock down the historical evidence
for the resurrection of Jesus, which have finished
in happy disaster! The Christian writer Roger
Forster recalls one of them like this: 'In the
eighteenth century a couple of men decided,
when they went up to Oxford, that they would
share the attack between them. Lord Lyttleton
would write a book to prove that the apostle
Paul was never actually converted to Jesus Christ
(a bold attempt, if nothing else!); the other man,
Gilbert West, decided that he would attack the
resurrection, the fundamental plank of Christianity. So each set about his task, not meeting for
some years. When at last they met, and asked
how each was getting on with his respective
work, Lyttleton said, in effect, that he was sorry,
but he was just not going to get the book out.
In fact, as he had studied the material to try and

weigh up the case, he himself had been converted
to Christ. He was sorry to disappoint his friend!
Gilbert West replied that, as a matter of fact, he
had written his book but it would be coming out
as a book in *defence of the resurrection of Jesus.*
You can find the book today in the British
Museum, and on the fly-leaf there is a quotation
from the Book of Ecclesiasticus (in the Apocry-
pha), and it says, "Don't judge a matter until
you have examined it." '[10]

Much the same thing happened to the twentieth-century American lawyer Frank Morison.
He started out to write against the resurrection,
but the opening chapter of the book he did
eventually write is entitled 'The book that
refused to be written'. He, too, had been convinced of the resurrection of Jesus. This is the
strength of the historical evidence which anyone can investigate.

But there is a second and much more direct
way of investigating the truth of Christ's resurrection. For many of us, if we had to choose the
disciple to whom we most closely relate, it would
be doubting Thomas. There is something so
practical and straight about the man. He never
hid his doubts. He would not believe anything
until he had seen the evidence.

The other disciples were in a great mood of
joy and expectation, saying that they had met
the risen Lord Jesus Christ. Thomas, however,
had not seen him. He had not been there when
Jesus came to the others. So he said, 'Unless I
see the nail marks in his hands and put my finger
where the nails were, and put my hand into his

side, I will not believe.'

There is plenty of doubt there. There is, however, also something else in what he said. 'Unless I see, I will not believe.' The implication is 'If I am confronted with the proof, I will believe. If the living Lord Jesus Christ would meet with me, then I will most certainly believe.'

The second way in which you can investigate the Christian claim that Jesus is alive from the dead is the test of personal experience. If Jesus is really alive, he can meet with people now. The risen Christ can be tested in your own life when you come to the point where you can sincerely pray, 'Lord Jesus, if you are there, and you make yourself known to me, then I will follow you.' The way to certainty is to add personal encounter with the living Christ to the sure foundation of historical evidence. You have the doubt of Thomas, but do you have the honesty of Thomas? Are you prepared to be open to Christ?

There is a man in Northern Ireland, a 'Protestant', who had carried out a sectarian murder. The police had absolutely no clue at all as to who was the culprit. One day he walked into a police station and gave himself up. The police were totally staggered. 'Why?' they asked, 'No one suspected you, why on earth did you give yourself up?' The man's answer was 'My life has been changed by Jesus Christ. The living Lord Jesus Christ has come into my life, and now I must do what is right.' Jesus is alive, and he is able to make himself known *that* definitely in people's lives today.

The relevance of the resurrection

What is the relevance of the resurrection of the
Lord Jesus Christ to the problem of suffering
and death which we began to consider at the
beginning of this chapter? The answer is that it
assures us of God's final solution to suffering.
The factual, bodily resurrection of Jesus shows
us quite plainly that heaven and life after death
are not just a load of comforting twaddle, just a
lot of pie in the sky. Eternal life is real. Heaven
is real.

The Bible declares that eventually God will
make a new heaven and a new earth. In that
place there will be a vast multitude of people
who have trusted Christ. In that place there will
be no more suffering, there are no more tears,
no more death, nor sorrow, nor sobbing, nor any
more pain. Heaven is God's ultimate answer to
man's suffering. It may not be the answer which
we would have expected, but the resurrection
of Christ indicates that it is the true and final
answer.

Now, what makes this so interesting is the
way people get to heaven. How do people get to
that place of no more suffering? If we were able
to ask them, they would all give one answer.
They would all point back to one man's *suffering:* the suffering of Jesus on the cross to take
away their sin. How do men and women come
to that place of no more death? They would
answer by pointing to one man's *death:* the
death of the Lord Jesus Christ, the just dying for
the unjust to bring us to God. This all shows yet

again the marvellous power and wisdom and love of God. God has taken the greatest bane of mankind, human suffering, and turned it round through the suffering of Jesus Christ, to produce the greatest blessing of mankind — the open door to heaven and eternal life!

What is the answer to suffering? God himself has suffered in the person of Jesus Christ in order that we might never suffer again. God is truly concerned that people should be delivered from suffering and death. 'Do I take any pleasure in the death of the wicked? declares the Sovereign Lord. Rather, am I not pleased when they turn from their ways and live?' (Ezekiel 18:23.) God has provided the way of escape, through the cross of Jesus, for all who put their trust in him and trust their lives into his hands.

The issues involved here are profound, and must not be minimized. Everything is at stake in this matter. Jesus *is* the answer to death, but if you will not have Jesus then you are choosing eternal death. The Bible makes plain something which Christians find very difficult to say to people, but which is nevertheless true. Jesus Christ *is* the way to ultimate deliverance from suffering, but if we will not have Jesus then we are choosing eternal suffering. Jesus said, 'Enter through the narrow gate. For wide is the gate and broad is the road that leads to destruction, and many enter through it. But small is the gate and narrow the road that leads to life, and only a few find it' (Matthew 7:13,14).

What practical relevance does this fact of the resurrection have for people here and now? The

practical outworking of this is that it releases
Christians from the fear of death. Looking at the
resurrection of Jesus, Christians can know that
there is life after death, and *they,* through their
being joined to Jesus by faith, have nothing to
fear. Jesus said, 'I am the resurrection and the
life. He who believes in me will live, even though
he dies' (John 11: 25).

Let me give you three testimonies of Christians
as they faced death. They are very different
people culturally, from very different parts
of the world, but all with one thing in common,
their faith in Christ.

The first was a young English doctor, James
Casson, a family man, who in his mid-thirties,
with life before him, was found to have terminal
cancer. He was a Christian, and in his last months
before his death in June 1980, he was able to
write a little booklet with the title, *Dying, the
greatest adventure of my life.* As you read what
he says, remember these are not the words of
some preacher far removed from the situation;
these are the words of a man who knows that *he*
is dying. 'I believe that there is no ground for
fear of death and what comes after. The process
of dying is one of which I do sometimes become
fearful, and this is a natural reaction experienced,
I believe, even by our Lord himself in Geth-
semane. But the freedom from fear of death itself is even more liberating when it is seen in the
biblical context. Forgiveness lies in a personal
acceptance of the death of Christ on our behalf,
not just as a man would die for his country or
his family, but as the Son of God dying for a sin-

ful person that is me. Once such a step has been
taken hope begins to take shape and once the
underlying truth of the resurrection has been
understood the real wonder of it becomes crystal
clear. This new life becomes ours, only a shadow
now but after death to go on for ever. The choice
is ours. All the facts are available to us. God's
judgement will be manifestly fair, most of all to
those who are judged. This is not easy to accept,
but I can promise each and every one who takes
such a step of faith that any fear of death will
go.' ' . . . What are my feelings as I write these
final paragraphs? Firstly, surprise that I have
survived long enough to finish it. Some days I
have felt so ill it seemed I could not possibly
awake the next morning. Secondly, a conviction
that even if one person benefits through it the
effort will have been worthwhile. Thirdly, the
unceasing awareness of the spiritual world as my
body weakens, of music on a distant hill becoming louder, of the vision of glory becoming more
clear now that my journey is almost over.'[11]

The second person whose Christian experience
as he faced death says so much is Josif Ton. He
is a native of Rumania and was threatened with
death by the authorities in that country because
of his Christian faith. 'I was taken one day in
1977 and charged with treason and conspiracy
to commit treason. For that the punishment is
death. I was taken in front of the Minister of the
Interior and he told me he was going to shoot
me. "But before that," he said, "I'll burn you,
I'll torture you." And then I was taken from his
office to the place where they had been interrog-

ating me, and the major who had been interrog-
ating me said, "Mr Ton, can't you see they
are going to shoot you? Do something to save
your life." I said, "What shall I do to save my
life?" He said, "I think, if you confess that all
these papers that you wrote last year, that you
wrote them at the command of your masters in
the West, if you ask for forgiveness and promise
that you will not write like that any more, they
will spare your life." I smiled and said, "Sir,
what you propose to me is spiritual suicide.
I prefer the physical death. But I tell you there
is no need for me to save my life; you just go on
and shoot me." I never saw a more furious man
in my life, because you can't do anything to a
man who says, "Shoot me." '[12]

Josif goes on to tell of another Christian,
similarly threatened with death, who was able
to say this: 'When you threaten me with death,
actually you say that you will send me to glory,
and you can't threaten me with glory!' The
Christian faith really does enable people to face
death without fear.

The third testimony comes from Africa, in
Uganda in 1973, when the regime of Idi Amin
was in power. Bishop Festo Kivengere describes
what happened one day as he was asked to
attend the execution of three men. 'February 10
began as a sad day for us in Kabale. People were
commanded to come to the stadium and witness
the execution by firing squad of the three young
men of our area. Death permeated the atmosphere in that stadium. A silent crowd of about
three thousand was there to watch the spectacle.

'I had permission from the authorities to speak to the men before they died, and two of my fellow ministers were with me. They brought the men in a truck and unloaded them. They were handcuffed and their feet were chained. The firing squad stood at attention. As we walked away into the centre of the stadium, I was wondering what to say to these men in the few minutes we had before their death. How do you give the gospel to doomed men who are probably seething with rage?

'We approached them from behind, and as they turned round to look at us, what a sight! Their faces were alight with an unmistakable glow and radiance. Before we could say anything, one of them burst out: "Bishop, thank you for coming! I wanted to tell you. The day I was arrested, in my prison cell, I asked the Lord Jesus to come into my heart. He came in and forgave all my sins! Heaven is now open, and there is nothing between me and God! Please tell my wife and children that I am going to be with Jesus. Ask them to accept him into their lives as I did."

'The second man told us a similar story, excitedly raising his hands, which rattled the handcuffs. Then the youngest said: "I once knew the Lord, but I went away from him and got into political confusion. After I was arrested, I came back to the Lord. He has forgiven me and filled me with peace. Please tell my parents . . . and warn my younger brothers never to go away from the Lord Jesus."

'I felt that what I needed to do was to talk to

the soldiers, not to the condemned. So I trans-
lated what the men had said into a language the
soldiers understood. The military men were
standing there with their guns cocked, and bewil-
derment on their faces. Those in the stadium
who were near enough could hear it too, and the
rest could see the radiance on the faces of the
condemned which showed they were forgiven
souls.

'The soldiers were so dumbfounded at the
faces and words of the men they were about to
execute that they even forgot to put the hoods
over their faces! The three faced the firing squad
standing close together. They looked toward the
people and began to wave, handcuffs and all.
The people waved back. Then shots were fired
and the three were with Jesus.

'We stood in front of them, our hearts throb-
bing with joy, mingled with tears. It was a day
never to be forgotten. Though dead the men
spoke loudly to all of Kigeze district and beyond,
so that there was an upsurge of life in Christ,
which challenges death and defeats it . . .

'We heard that the soldiers who were in the
firing squad and the guards standing by could
not shake off the reality of what they saw — the
glory of God on the faces of dying men.'[13]

Christ is alive. He is the final answer to all
suffering and death. He has died for the sins of
all who believe in him and has put them right
with God, so that they need no longer fear death.
'God . . . raised him from the dead and glorified
him and so your faith and hope are in God'
(1 Peter 1:21).

4.
Can religion really help?

In 1971 an object was displayed in a museum in County Durham as being a Roman coin, minted between A.D. 135 and 138. However, a young girl, aged nine, entering the museum and seeing this item, went to the keepers of the museum and pointed out that in fact it was a plastic token given away free by a soft drinks firm in exchange for bottle labels! A spokesman for the museum later commented, 'The trouble was that we construed the letter "R" on the coin to mean "Roma". In fact it stood for "Robinsons", the soft drink manufacturers.'[14] In most things in life there is the real and there is the plastic imitation!

'I see the relevance of Christianity, but if I became a Christian it must be genuine with me. I couldn't stand to be someone simply carrying on a pretence, all words but no reality.' These were the sentiments of someone I know who was standing on the brink of Christian faith. Having seen hypocritical religion, it is a fear which understandably arises in people's minds. Nobody wants to be a Pharisee. It is this difference between just having 'religion' and actually knowing the living and true God, which is a vital issue.

Religion

This distinction between religion and reality is
certainly a distinction which Jesus made. 'Now
there was a man of the Pharisees named Nicodemus, a member of the Jewish ruling council.
He came to Jesus at night and said, "Rabbi, we
know you are a teacher who has come from God.
For no one could perform the miraculous signs
you are doing if God were not with him." In
reply Jesus declared, "I tell you the truth,
unless a man is born again, he cannot see the
kingdom of God" ' (John 3:1-3).

This man Nicodemus was an intellectual
religious teacher. He was also a very sincere man;
that is why he was honest enough to come and
talk to Jesus about knowing God, rather than
dismissing him out of hand, like the rest of the
Pharisees.

He was serious, he was sincere, but Jesus'
loving estimate of him was 'Nicodemus, you
have only got religion; you haven't got a real
relationship with God; you need to be born
again.' It was the same with the apostle Paul
before he met Christ: he was zealous, fervent,
dedicated, but not saved.

For people who only have 'religion', their
experience is not a satisfying relationship with
God. It is empty religion. So we ask ourselves,
'Well, why on earth do people get mixed up in
empty religion?' 'What do they carry on with
it for?'

I believe that the answer is fear. The root of
'religion' is fear. Let me introduce you to two

people and suggest to you how this terrible bondage of empty religion works.

The first person we will call 'Mr Escapist'. Many people are afraid of life with all its difficulties and afraid of death. This is the situation with Mr Escapist. Deep down this man does not believe in God at all. Deep down he still accepts the materialistic world-view which says that there is only this life with all its rough edges, and nothing else. Mr Escapist, however, cannot face what he sees as the harsh reality of such an outlook, so he escapes into a fantasy world of 'religion'. This is where the futurist writer Alvin Toffler locates much religion today, against the background of our fast-changing society which puts so many pressures on the individual that people feel they cannot cope. 'Instead of constructing a new culture appropriate to the new world, they attempt to import and implant old ideas appropriate to other times and places or to revive the fanatic faiths of their own ancestors who lived under radically different conditions.'[15]

The organized Christian church, along with many other religious bodies, has to take such comments on the chin. Yes, there are people in the churches like Mr Escapist, who simply have religion. What then does the Bible say about that? It agrees that there are people who make gods of their imagination. They escape by manufacturing the strange state of consciousness produced by Transcendental Meditation, or whatever. They have religion, but they have no contact with the living and true God. In fact, the Bible is quite derisive about those who manu-

facture their own gods, when the living God is
there to be known. 'Their idols are silver and gold,
made by the hands of men. They have mouths,
but cannot speak, eyes, but they cannot see . . .
Those who make them will be like them, and so
will all who trust in them' (Psalm 115:4-8).

Here is Mr Escapist, with his little fantasy
world of religion, and Jesus says to him, 'Nicodemus, you may be religious, but you do not
know God.'

The second person with a religion based on
fear, we will call Mrs Traditionalist. She is a lady
who accepts the idea of God, probably because
she was brought up to it by her parents, but has
never truly grasped the gospel of God's love and
free pardon in Jesus Christ. Not knowing God's
love, she is afraid of God. She is afraid to have
God come into her life. She is afraid of what
that might mean, so she keeps it all at arm's
length. She is afraid to have God at the controls
of her life. She keeps the steering-wheel of her
life very much in her own hands. The mark of
her religion is that, because she does not really
know the Lord, she has no true peace of heart
and mind. For all her religious observance, she
has no peace of conscience, but simply fear of
God's justice and power.

This was the experience of Martin Luther,
before he found Christ. He was living as a very
religious monk, trying to live by the stringent
monastic rules. 'I tried as hard as I could to keep
the Rule. I used to be contrite, and make a list
of my sins. I confessed them again and again.
I scrupulously carried out the penances which

were allotted to me. And yet my conscience kept nagging. It kept telling me, "You fell short there." "You were not sorry enough." "You left that sin off your list." I was trying to cure the doubts and scruples of the conscience with human remedies, the traditions of men. The more I tried these remedies, the more troubled and uneasy my conscience grew.'[16]

At one point, Luther is so blunt and honest. Caught up in this empty religion, he says that because he never had any real peace of heart, he used to hate God rather than love him. He was tormented by fear. 'Nicodemus,' says Jesus, 'you are a very honest man, you are a very sincere man, but you do not know God.' All these people have is religion based on fear, not the tremendous privilege of a true relationship with God.

Reality

What is the great mark of a real relationship with God? What does the real thing look like?

When Jesus entered history he brought with him almost a new name for God, a name that had lain virtually undiscovered in its full meaning. The name was 'Father'. He referred to God as his own Father in a special way. But he also referred to God as the Christian's Father.

Throughout the Sermon on the Mount, Jesus keeps referring to God as the Father of those who follow him. How is the Christian to behave? Jesus does not give a great list of rules and regu-

lations, but he simply emphasizes that we are to
imitate our heavenly Father. And what is the
motive for such behaviour? It is love for our
Father, who has so loved us.

What is the great mark of a real relationship
with God? It is that through the work of the
Lord Jesus Christ people actually do come to
know that God is *their* Father. They know that
he loves them like a Father, and they love him
as their Father.

After Jesus was raised from the dead, he
returned to heaven, promising that he would
send the Holy Spirit to dwell in the hearts of his
disciples. What great work did the Holy Spirit
come to do in the hearts of Christians? The
apostle Paul puts it like this: 'You did not receive
a spirit that makes you a slave again to fear, but
you received the Spirit of sonship. And by him
we cry, "*Abba,* Father" ' (Romans 8:15). '*Abba*'
is an Aramaic word (Jesus' native language) for
'Dad'. The Christian, says Paul, knows and
experiences God as his or her Father. This great
change takes place from slavish fear of God to
faith and reverent trust in our Father. A Christian comes to *love* God from the heart.

Bilquis Sheikh, a Muslim woman, described
how she truly found the Lord. She had been
brought up in the religion of Islam, in which
God is pictured as a distant, faraway, stern figure
to whom you just have the duty to submit. She
became a Christian, and discovered to her great
joy the true God through faith in Jesus. She
wrote down her story in a book, and the title of
the book sums up the wonderful reality which

she found about God: it is called *I Dared to Call Him Father.* [17] Knowing God is not a tedious religion of fear, it is a deep and holy and joyful relationship with Father. Even in times of trouble the Christian can be assured that his Father has it all under control. The parent-child relationship with God can bring a profound peace and strength to our lives.

A girl, who found God after being brought up in formal Roman Catholic religion, explained the change that had occurred in her life like this: 'Now I have a personal relationship with God. He is real. Before there was no need as everything was done for you; no need to pray yourself or ask God's forgiveness for yourself — in the Catholic church the priest supposedly does it all for you. As a Christian I have a whole new idea of God as Father. I am able to approach him myself with no people between us . . . When I was a Catholic I never felt I could be totally rid of my sin; there was no assurance of forgiveness . . . If people ask me now, 'What is a Christian?' I would tell them, "Someone who has a personal relationship with God." '

The apostle John writes about the Christian like this: 'How great is the love the Father has lavished on us, that we should be called children of God! And that is what we are! The reason the world does not know us is that it did not know him. Dear friends, now we are children of God . . . ' (1 John 3:1, 2).

How can we find God? How can we find the reality of knowing God as our own Father? We need to look at the New Testament for the answer to that question.

When Jesus left off being a carpenter and
began to preach, his message was this: 'The time
has come, the kingdom of God is near. [So]
repent and believe the good news!' (Mark 1:15.)
When the apostle Paul, who had seen many
people come to be children of God under his
ministry, was summing up what he had preached
to them, he said this: 'I have declared to both
Jews and Greeks that they must turn to God in
repentance and have faith in our Lord Jesus'
(Acts 20:21).

Jesus says, 'Repent and believe.' Paul says,
'Repent and believe.' The way to God is through
repentance and faith.

Repentance

Repentance begins with a person owning up and
being honest about his sin and waywardness.
There can be no true repentance without a person coming to realize that he or she has failed to
live the kind of life that is pleasing to God, and
that this failure is his or her fault. Repentance
begins when a person is prepared honestly and
with sorrow to admit, 'I'm in the wrong.'

In our society, we see all kinds of pressures to
quench that admission. The bosses blame the
unions and the unions blame the bosses. The
teachers blame the parents and the parents
blame the teachers. No one wants to say, 'It was
my fault.'

> I went to my psychiatrist
> to be psychoanalysed
> to find out why I killed the cat
> and blackened my wife's eyes.
>
> He put me on a downy couch
> to see what he could find
> and this is what he dredged up
> from my subconscious mind.
>
> When I was one, my mummy hid
> my dolly in the trunk
> and so it follows naturally
> that I am always drunk.
>
> When I was two, I saw my father
> kiss the maid one day
> and that is why I suffer now
> from kleptomania.
>
> When I was three, I suffered from
> ambivalence towards my brothers,
> so it follows naturally
> I poisoned all my lovers.
>
> I'm so glad that I have learned
> that lesson it has taught
> that everything I do that's wrong
> is someone else's fault.[18]

Of course, that poem is an exaggerated version of how our society thinks. But the repentant man, the repentant woman says, 'No, it's *my* fault. I am the one to blame. Away with all this continual excusing of everybody. I did it, I'm wrong.' The repentant person confesses to God, 'Lord, my life is a mess, and my life is just offensive to you, and it is my fault.' Jesus spoke of two men who went to the temple to pray, one of whom could see nothing that he had to confess; if anybody was wrong it was other people. Jesus said he prayed to himself; God was not listening to him. There was another man there, who felt his sin so deeply, all he could do was pray, 'God be merciful to me a sinner.' The man was saying, 'Lord, I know I've done wrong, thought wrong, am wrong. Lord, I've got nothing to commend me to you. Please simply have mercy upon me.' Jesus said that God listened to that repentant man, and he was saved (Luke 18:13,14).

But repentance does not stop at just admitting you are wrong. It involves more than confession; it involves action. When Laker Airways went bust in 1982, one Laker plane had started out from Manchester Airport, and while in mid-flight the news broke that the company was finished. The plane had to turn around in mid-flight and come back. Repentance is not only admitting that your life is bankrupt in God's sight and that it is your fault. Repentance involves a turn round from self-centred living to God-centred living. We have been living our lives according to what we want. Repentance is to turn round and start living for God. We cannot have God and keep sin in our lives. It simply will not work. If we are to turn to God, we must turn away from sin.

Repentance means a changed life. That grudge,

that perhaps you have held against your parents, will have to be dropped and replaced by genuine respect and care. That kick, that perhaps you get out of baiting people and making them feel small, will have to go. The way you use Sunday, the day for God's worship, will have to change. That self-pity, in which you love to bathe and wallow, that gnawing love for more and more material possessions must be replaced by profound and reverent love for the Father. Jesus said to a woman caught in the act of adultery, 'Go and sin no more' (John 8:11). A repentant person will do all he or she can to make a clean break with sin so as to please God. Repentance involves a person honestly saying to God. 'O Lord, I know I'll never be perfect in this life, but Father please enable me to make a clean break with the way I have lived my life up till now, so as to live for you.' God's power is greater than the power of sin. You know that sin has a grip upon you which you cannot break. But God *can* deliver you from it dominating your life.

Repentance means a changed life. The changed life will not be easy. To follow Christ involves trouble. All easy religion is false religion. Do you know why? Because the world is alienated from God, and if you really become a child of God, the world will be alienated from you, too. Are you ready for that? 'Sit down,' says Jesus, 'and count the cost.' The way is narrow, but the destination more than makes up for it. 'For who-ever wants to save his life will lose it, but who-ever loses his life for me and for the gospel will save it. What good is it for a man to gain the

whole world, yet forfeit his soul? Or what can a
man give in exchange for his soul?' (Mark 8:
35-37.) Says Jesus, the richest people, who have
lived the most comfortable and untroubled lives,
will suffer eternal loss, having rejected him.
Whereas those who have taken up the cross and
followed Jesus in this life will know not only all
the comfort of the Holy Spirit in this life, but all
the blessings of God for ever.

Here we have begun to sketch out something
of what it means when the Bible speaks of
repentance towards God.

Faith

Over five hundred times the New Testament
directs us towards faith. This faith is to be
centred specifically on Jesus and his cross. Let
us go again to the scene of the crucifixion.

'They brought Jesus to the place called Golgotha (which means the Place of the Skull).
Then they offered him wine mixed with myrrh,
but he did not take it. And they crucified
him . . .

'At the sixth hour darkness came over the
whole land until the ninth hour. And at the
ninth hour Jesus cried out in a loud voice,
"Eloi, Eloi, lama sabachthani?" — which means
"My God, my God, why have you forsaken
me?" . . .

'With a loud cry, Jesus breathed his last.

'The curtain of the temple was torn in two
from top to bottom. And when the centurion,

who stood there in front of Jesus, heard his cry
and saw how he died, he said, "Surely this man
was the Son of God!" ' (Mark 15:22-39.)

The teaching of the New Testament is that on
the cross Jesus did *everything* necessary to put
us right with God. Because of our sins, the ways
we have thought and acted, we deserve to be
forsaken by God. But on the cross Jesus was
forsaken by God, in our place. That is why he
cried, *'Eloi, Eloi, lama sabachthani?'* When Jesus
died the veil which excluded people from the
most holy part of the Jewish temple was torn
down. The veil covered the place where God's
manifest presence, his glory, had been seen in
former days. No one had been allowed to enter
there. But at the death of Jesus that veil is torn
down, symbolizing the fact that the way into
God's presence is now open to all. All that was
required to enable us to come to God was accom-
plished for us by Jesus on the cross.

Faith is simply trusting Christ to bring *you* to
God. No longer to rely on what a nice person
you think you are, no longer to rely on your
own honesty, no longer to rely on your church-
going or what you see as your own sincerity, but
simply to rely wholly on Jesus. When a person
comes to Christ, it bears many parallels with
what happens when two people get married. We
are the bride and Christ is the husband. The
bride, at the time of marriage, gives herself to
her husband, to trust, to follow, and says in
effect, I am no longer my own but I belong to
you. The husband responds by taking the bride
to protect, to care for, to love and provide for,

and give himself for her good. Christ has laid
down his life for all who trust him. What better
husband could there possibly be? *You* should
place all *your* life in his hands for ever. Seek him
in the humble and dependent attitude of a man
who once said to Jesus, 'I do believe; help me to
overcome my unbelief!' (Mark 9:24.) Seek him
in prayer that you should enter into such a marriage with Christ. Trust him for everything. This
is the way to God.

When Martin Luther turned from his sin in
repentance, and put his faith in Christ, he realized
that he was saved, that he was one of God's own
children. He wrote, 'When I realized this I felt
myself absolutely born again; the gates of para-
dise had been flung open and I had entered!'[19]

How does a person become a Christian in practice? We have seen the great principles which the Bible lays down as the only foundation for coming to the Lord. But how does a person find Christ in the 1980s? Here are the stories of two people who came to trust the Lord Jesus. They are included with the hope that they will help others to find him, too.

5.
Two real-life stories: Sandra

I was born in 1948 in Gloucestershire, the elder
of two girls. Our home was not Christian. My
father claimed to be a believer but my mother
had no time for religion and confessed to being
an atheist. The result was that my parents often
had bitter rows on the subject, which bred in me
a suspicion of, and aversion to, religious matters.
I was, however, sent to a Baptist Sunday School.
Although I can remember precious little of those
years, I like to think that it was here that some
seeds of truth were sown. At least I was exposed
to the Scriptures, and this was to be the only
form of spiritual teaching that I was to receive
until the year of my conversion.

When I was ten we moved to the Midlands and,
apart from the questionable content of school
assemblies and Religious Education classes, I had
no contact with religion at all. I didn't go to
church, except for the occasional wedding. I
never felt I could belong in a church environ-
ment and never wanted to. School was my life.
I loved school and thrived on it. I was genuinely
heart-broken when my school-days came to an
end.

When I was seventeen my mother left home
for another man. My parents had never been
happy together, so it did not come as too much
of a surprise. But it was still a great shock. In
those days divorce was not so common or so
socially acceptable as it is today, and it was a
distressing and humiliating time. The family was
split; I stayed with my father and my sister went
to live with my mother.

I went from school to university to study for
a degree in Biological Sciences. I was glad to get
away from the home that no longer existed and
start a life on my own. I concentrated on having
a good time and on getting through with the
minimum of work. I was successful in both. My
spiritual life remained dead during my university
years, though I was foolish enough to read some
of Dennis Wheatley's books on black magic.
They aroused in me a morbid interest and curiosity in the occult which stayed with me until I
became free in Christ. I was awakened to the
existence of the force of evil in the world and
became Satan-fearing. It was a logical step, using
the science law of equal and opposite forces, to
have to admit to the existence of a power of
good and light, and I noticed in the books that
good always triumphed over evil. But this was
just a general observation and brought me no
nearer to knowing God.

By the time my education was finished I was
well indoctrinated with the evolution theory.
Though nowadays people are perhaps not quite
so dogmatic in its teaching, to me it was taught
as fact from early school-days. If anyone had

tried seriously to put forward a case for creation, I would have laughed scornfully and put them down as religious nutcases! Later I was to have to undergo a huge U-turn in my understanding of the origins of life.

During my final year at university I met the man whom I was to marry the following year. In 1970 we graduated and moved to London, my husband's home town. I hated London from the outset and never managed to adjust fully to city life. I am ashamed to say that we married in church. We were both unbelievers and it was hypocritical. God had not had any part in the making of that marriage; we just gatecrashed into one of his houses for the sense of occasion and ceremony, like actors stepping into a film set.

The first years of marriage were very happy. Like most young couples around us, we both worked and saved hard towards buying our own home. Starting a family was out of the question until we had amassed a certain amount of material possessions. But gradually, as we achieved our ambitions in the material sense, and as my hatred of London grew more intense, I started to become unhappy in my marriage and discontented with life in general. I was still interested in the occult. I took astrology very seriously and avidly scanned the "stars" in the hope of seeing a brighter future. This preoccupation deepened as I got more depressed and miserable. I consulted fortune-tellers and tarot-card readers. But I found little comfort for my misery. I always came away feeling more miserable and with more questions unanswered than had been answered.

We finally got a home that we were proud of, but I was no more content than before. I had the material things around me that I had wanted and had striven for, but my life seemed empty. It was as if the joy had been in the striving for a goal, but once achieved the goal no longer seemed worth having. Something important was missing.

I was still spiritually unawakened but in 1976 something happened to rouse me. On Christmas Eve of that year my grandmother died. She was my father's mother and the only grandparent I had known and loved. This was my first experience of death. Gran was buried on a cold, wet New Year's Eve. There had been a moving service in the small local Baptist Church to which Gran had belonged. I know now that my Gran was a Christian and I rejoice to know she is now with her Saviour. But these things were alien to me then. I was deeply affected by the burial service. I remember standing on the edge of the grave, watching the coffin being lowered into the cold, unfriendly earth. I hated it. Everything inside me welled up to scream against it. I refused to believe that my Gran was in that coffin. I knew she was still alive somewhere. I found myself believing in the existence of the spirit and of some sort of life after death. I was very confused. I wanted to know the truth and had many questions I wanted answering. I began a search for that truth that was to last me four years, until God in his mercy reached down and made me his.

In 1977 I left my husband. I couldn't stand it

any more. I was unhappy at work, unhappy in my marriage and hated London. I was also involved in a brief extramarital relationship that, although not serious, was yet another symptom of an unhappy life. I needed to get away and sort myself out. I had worked for seven years as a laboratory technician. I now looked for job opportunities outside London. I was successful at my first attempt, gaining employment with promotion at Surrey University in Guildford. I moved there with the intention that my husband would perhaps follow later if things between us improved once I was away from London. But they didn't improve and I soon realized that I wanted to go it alone. It wasn't easy as I had to start at the bottom again — back to bed-sit life. After two years of separation I started divorce proceedings. There was no resistance from my husband and I obtained the decree absolute in 1980. It was the second time in my life that I experienced divorce in my family. It is a hideous, painful thing and something from which one never really recovers; there are always some scars left.

When I started my new life I found out what it meant to be lonely. In London I had had a busy social life and I suffered greatly from being cut off from all my friends. It wasn't easy learning to be independent after six sheltered years of married life. Even simple things like going into a coffee shop took on terrifying proportions. One night I was having a good cry, feeling very sorry for myself, and I just sobbed out, 'Dear God, please help me.' But that was all I could manage.

I didn't know how to pray. I didn't know then
that praying was just talking to God.

In my search for answers to my spiritual
questions I took myself down several blind
alleys. I can only thank God that he kept me
safe during this time. My mother had become a
believer in spiritualism and for a while I was
interested in finding out what it had to offer.
On several occasions when I visited her we
would attend spiritualist meetings together.
I went mainly out of curiosity and wasn't very
impressed. I found it all a bit pathetic, as a large
number of those who went seemed to be lonely
people seeking a message or word of comfort
from loved ones on the 'other side'. The emphasis
seemed to be on supernatural happenings, such
as spirit manifestations, automatic writing or
drawing, foretelling the future and so on. There
was nothing there to satisfy a hungry soul and I
soon lost interest. I had no idea then as to the
danger I was in spiritually.

On another occasion I went with a friend,
who was also interested in the occult, to a place
in London where we had made appointments
to see a clairvoyant. I found the experience terrifying. It was an aggressive interview during
which I was bombarded with information and
facts about myself that were all true. She got the
past events correct, but her portrayal of my
future was all wrong. I came away feeling shaken
and, again, no nearer knowing peace.

I eventually found myself a boyfriend and my
loneliness, at least, was no longer a problem. I
was to stay with him for the next three years,

until my conversion. Life settled down and became less desperate. I tried hard to get 'religious'. I started to read my Bible, but it was difficult. It was like trying to cope with a dry old history book.

My spiritual searchings now went down more orthodox channels. I was reading 'religious' books but they all had a Roman Catholic influence. I became very interested in Mother Theresa and her work among the lepers in India. I was also interested in reading about the saints, St Francis of Assisi in particular. My boyfriend was a Roman Catholic though he no longer practised his faith. I got him to take me along to a couple of services to see what they were like. Although I enjoyed it to a certain extent, and was impressed with the outward show of friendship extended one to another, I was not 'hooked'. I tried to accept Roman Catholicism because I felt that as a religion it had stood the test of time, so there had to be something there. But as I looked beneath the surface I found things I couldn't accept. One was all the apparent wealth of the church, in stark contrast to the dreadful poverty of many of its members. I was offended by the practice of confession, at least to another human being. I could not see how any man could have the power to absolve sins. Surely that was something only God could do? Besides, confession seemed to be taken very lightly by Catholics. It seemed pointless to me to confess some misdemeanour only to feel free to go and do the same thing again. I was appalled too at the lack of respect shown by some people in church, notably those who attended while under the influence of drink. No, Roman Catholicism was not for me.

After two years working at Surrey University I was to change my occupation. There is no time here to tell how it happened, but I am sure that God had a hand in it, as the change of occupation was drastic and one which I had never before contemplated. I went into nursing. I started as an auxiliary but took to it so quickly that I applied to train as a State Registered Nurse almost as soon as I had started. I loved nursing and came to regard it as a great privilege. The first time I found myself on my knees washing and drying a patient's feet the thought came to me, 'I wish these were Jesus' feet.' I seemed to recall a story in the Bible where a woman wept over Jesus' feet and dried them with her hair. And he had said to her, 'Your sins are forgiven.' This was important to me. As I was gradually becoming more conscious of God, I was becoming more aware of my own sinfulness. The guilt of my marriage failure especially lay heavy on my conscience.

When I started my training there were many adjustments to make. I was thirty-one years old and my fellow students were mostly eighteen. I was worried how I would fit in. But God had it all taken care of! He blessed me in my friend Jenny, who started her training at the same time and who was also a 'mature' student. We naturally gravitated to seeking each other's company and over the months our friendship deepened. We used to have many discussions together and the topic of religion would often crop up. We both felt a need to belong to a church, but the problem was which one should we try. To an outsider there are so many to choose from, and we didn't want to get involved in anything 'freaky'. We never did make a decision for ourselves; it was made for us. We attended one of Cliff Richard's gospel concerts in aid of TEAR Fund. I found it very moving and later bought Cliff's book *Which One's Cliff?* in order to read about his conversion to Christianity. I was reading the book one lunch-time in the canteen at the hospital. Laurel, a midwifery student and a stranger to me, came up to sit with me and started talking about Cliff. Laurel asked me if I went to church and when I said 'No' she invited me to go along with her one day. Although I wanted to, I was not very enthusiastic at first, as it was all happening a bit too quickly for me. I didn't like the feeling of things being taken out of my control and being 'arranged' for me. As it happened, I was unable to attend a Sunday service for several weeks, because of nursing duties. But I arranged with Laurel to go along to a Bible study and prayer evening. I was very nervous, as I'd never been to anything like this before and was worried about what I was letting myself in for. I will always remember that first night. The subject was the life of David. 'Oh no,' I groaned inwardly, 'boring Old Testament stuff.' But suddenly I was listening to Scripture that came alive, as it was expounded and brought up to date, in twentieth-century language. This time I was 'hooked', and I went back for more.

I was overcome, too, by the friendship that the church fellowship showed me. They seemed genuinely interested in me and showered me with kindness from the beginning. This in itself was something different in today's cold society.

My conversion came the night that I first heard the gospel preached; it was a baptismal service. By this time I had all the pieces of the jigsaw. I accepted God, Christ and the Bible as the Word of God, and I thought that was all there was to it. Was I in for a surprise!

I followed the pastor breathlessly through the doctrines of our faith: the original sin and resulting fall of man, the inherent sinfulness of all men and the necessity for Christ's death. For the first time in my life I understood why Christ had died and the meaning of the resurrection. The pastor explained the parables of the lost sheep and the prodigal son. As I followed him it all became personal. *I* was a lost sheep and Christ was there to take me back to the fold. He had died for me too! It was as if someone had switched on a light in a darkened room and all became clear to me. That was it. God had at last brought me home. My searching days were over. At last I knew where I was going and had the peace and assurance of sins forgiven. To my joy, my friend Jenny was converted the following week and we were eventually both baptized in that church.

I had a lot of sorting out to do in my life when I became a Christian and I could write a book of my experiences since then. But I have concentrated here on relevant events before my conversion as I feel this is more in line with the context of this book. Suffice it to say that I continue my walk with the Lord Jesus Christ, and the love that he gives his disciples more than compensates for anything that the world or its master Satan can throw at us. I have found God to be a bountiful provider for all needs and to be steadfast and sure in his love, however undeserving we may be. I no longer live in Guildford but in Wales. God has blessed me with a good Christian husband and we seek to serve him in our life together.

I leave you with part of Psalm 40 which had a special meaning for me at the beginning of my Christian life and which still says it all for me.

> He lifted me out of the slimy pit,
>   out of the mud and mire;
> he set my feet on a rock and gave
>   me a firm place to stand.
> He put a new song in my mouth,
>   a hymn of praise to our God.

Sandra Bowley
February 1985

Two real-life stories: Mike

I was born on 25 December 1941 in Hazelmere, Surrey and in 1945 my parents brought me to Pontefract, Yorkshire, where I have lived until now. My father was a worker at the nearby glass works and my mother cleaned the local school. I had an ordinary education — infant, junior and secondary modern (I failed the 11+ on purpose because it was considered 'cissy' to wear a grammar school uniform!), and I left school at the age of fifteen with no academic qualifications. I suppose it was about this time that I began to search for some meaning to life. I reconciled myself to not being 'brainy', but felt that I had sufficient intelligence to be able to make some serious investigations into the questions that were beginning to take on some more importance, such as, 'Who am I? Where do I fit into "the plan" (if there is such a plan) of life? How can you find happiness in a world where everybody else is looking for the same thing and consequently falling over each other and spoiling it for the rest — including me?' These thoughts, like dreams, surfaced unexpectedly and usually disappeared just as quickly! I would for the

most part just react to life on the emotional
level, almost instinctively you might say, prefer-
ring the *status quo* to any real thinking, absorb-
ing the views of others when they agreed with
me, disregarding them when they did not.

I would look at others to see if there were any
clues to answer my questions. The rich seemed
scared that others would steal their riches; the
poor never seemed to come to the end of their
labours, and when they did, they were just
thrown on the scrap heap of retirement. This led
to the cruelest blow of all: both rich and poor
could not avoid the last enemy, death.

When one looked at the famous, the well-to-
do, those in power, film stars, heroes, they all
alike, without exception, had skeletons in the
cupboard or fell from grace. The only way, it
seemed to me at the time, was to run away to
a desert island. Surely there I could be happy,
with no one else to interfere with my little life?
'But no,' I reasoned, I could not run away from
myself. My own feelings would pursue me even
there — anger, jealousy, envy and pride.

There were laws enough to govern society,
but no laws could govern the human heart; you
could not legislate for thoughts and attitudes.
People broke the laws, bent the laws and ignored
the laws. It became increasingly clear to me at
this time that no education, philosophy or
religion could change what was to me, even then,
the root of the problem — the human heart!

Religion seemed the worst confidence trick
of all, because it seemed to say, 'Do your best,
live a good life, do good to others and you will

be okay.' The problem was that while you were
busy doing these things, someone else would
kick you in the teeth. So I drifted along with my
contemporaries, living instinctively day to day
with not much thought for the future. I supposed
I would marry one day, after I had had my
'fling'. Being a teenager was an exciting experience. There were so many things to touch, see,
taste, but while grabbing all I could, I was
haunted by the nagging thought that it was all
meaningless.

Evolution, the theory that suggests that man
evolved from apes, held no certainties for me.
Even a brief survey of history proved to me
beyond doubt that man was no better now than
when he first began — whenever that was supposed to be!

Where did man get his moral attitude from?
Where did the idea of God come from? Why
was man not getting better? These questions
remained unanswered. Among the beer-drinking,
self-interested, gambling circles in which I
moved, 'Eat, drink and be merry, for tomorrow
we die,' seemed the only way to live! The only
problem was that many others had more than
me. Anyway, they would die too, so it worked
out equal in the end!

The years drifted by. I was married at 19. I
wanted companionship of a settled, secure type,
but all the time my own shortcomings and
imperfections kept getting in the way. Turning
over a new leaf always resulted in failure, so I
gave up trying. The idea of marriage as a partner-
ship of mutual love, trust and companionship

seemed foreign to the folk I lived among. 'Kitchen and kids, that's the place for the wife,' was a commonly held view, and yet my own marriage was no better, with me always the centre, and everybody else fitting in to *my* plans. I drifted in and out of jobs. I became a bus driver, the manager of a fish-and-chip shop, a tea-delivery man and a shop assistant. Somehow I was never able to settle down because at the back of my mind was the old problem of the seeming meaninglessness of it all in the face of death.

Work, pub, bed, day after day; work, TV, bed, for a change — so it went on. I was a good talker, so talked my way into what I considered to be a better job. I got a job as a sales representative. An expensive training programme in Stratford-upon-Avon, a car, commission, my own working hours — 'This is the life!' I thought. 'It will be different among the "better people".' But no. The same things went on there; only everything cost more! A large contract was taken from me by what turned out to be a subsidiary of the parent company I worked for. Management knew this all the time I was negotiating, but I was not told. When I did find out, I was furious and then totally disillusioned. So I went back to my old ways of escapism. I would avidly read science fiction books, instead of meeting prospective clients. I would go to the pictures or, worse, get drunk — anything to try and forget the meaninglessness of it all.

I was now in my mid-twenties, with two children, but my marriage was not a happy one.

I seemed unable to give myself to my wife and children as I wanted to. I was afraid and insecure. It seemed inevitable that we should drift apart. We were experiencing financial difficulties too — so much so that, to avoid creditors, my wife would come with me when my job took me to other counties. I eventually left the representative's job and went back to my old job of bus driving. At least there I would be out of the endless rat race. It was about this time that the first of three major events took place. A young woman, a close friend of the family, entered hospital for a routine operation, and died. I was devastated. Death came close for the first time in my life and I was shattered.

Suddenly I remembered the unkind, cruel things I had said to her, the cruel unkind thoughts about her, the things I could have said and should have said, the things I could have done, should have done and never did, and I was bitterly ashamed. My wife and I went to her funeral. I remember the church was packed and the young minister who took the service was in fact the minister who was later to be of such help to my wife and me.

Then shortly after this a second event took place. I had suffered from a bad chest for years (my mother died from TB) and I began to bleed from my right lung and was rushed into hospital. I thought I was going to die. They operated on me and removed a part of my right lung. I was told I had been in the operating theatre for seven hours. I was thirty years old.

As I began to recover, the enormity of what

had happened to me began to have an effect.
I remember one night, after visitors had gone,
walking down a corridor and looking out over
Leeds, seeing the people coming home, and
thinking, 'All this would still be going on if I
had died back there in the operating theatre.'
I prayed, I think properly for the first time in
my life: 'God, if you exist, then help me find
you!' I must confess, almost as soon as I got out
of hospital, I forgot that prayer, but God did not!

While still in hospital I did what I had always
done when I was troubled — I read. I remember
reading a book by the late Dennis Wheatley,
The Devil Rides Out. As I read this novel, I
became convinced of the power of evil in this
world that seeks to destroy men and women.
It wasn't only that book. Years of reading such
accounts — not all fictional — and an experience
with a ouija board were sufficient really to
frighten me. I longed for some assurance that
the opposite was true. To that end I sought the
advice of a clergyman who visited the hospital,
but all I could get from him was some vague
good wish for my speedy recovery — no affir-
mation of a power, person, or anything else that
would alleviate my now anxious, enquiring mind.
This further convinced me that organized religion had no real answers to anything. The only
good thing that came out of that episode was
that when I finally left hospital I was convinced
of a spiritual realm as never before.

As we began to pick up the threads of our
lives again, the third and, as it turned out, the
most significant event took place. Although I

had forgotten my prayer for help back there in the hospital, when I was again on the dole I would call in the local church on the way to 'sign on' and would pour out my troubles to a God I wasn't sure existed. The remarkable thing was that he answered, and a great many of my crises were dealt with — especially financial ones!

Along with many of my contemporaries, I was convinced that God, if he existed at all, couldn't pay the rent, feed and clothe the children, or do anything which occupied two-thirds of our lives. How foolish I was! During this time he did that and more, saving our entire home from being sold to pay off our debts! But even after all this I did not take him seriously, but just put him in my pocket with the thought that, if ever I needed him again, I could just bring him out, and, like Aladdin, rub the lamp of prayer and my God would answer. I remember what was to be my last visit to the church. Having gone in as usual, I began to speak to God, but something was dreadfully wrong. Instead of a certainty that he was listening, it was as if I were talking to a brick wall! I came out of that church a worried man. Why had he gone? What was wrong? I wrestled with these thoughts for some considerable time, but once again the 'real world' crowded in and I forgot my search.

It was at this time that we had begun to go out drinking with some friends, and one Saturday night their daughter agreed to baby-sit for us, providing I took her to her riding lesson early on Sunday morning. This I agreed to do and, having done so, I arrived home about

9 o'clock that morning. Imagine my surprise when I stepped into our lounge to see my wife and children dressed, and to be greeted with the words from my wife: 'I think it's about time the kids went to Sunday School'! A further remarkable thing happened: I found myself in total agreement with her! (We had never seriously discussed this with each other in the ten years of our marriage.) I had moved for years in circles where Sunday School was for middle-class namby-pambies. What's more, I, along with those circles, had always maintained that religion was something personal and you did not impose it on others, and certainly not on your children! They could make up their own minds later on — a bit like politics, sex, or death. You never talked about these things; they only brought arguments. Another thought crystallized in this incident: 'We cannot send the kids to Sunday School,' I said, 'and not go to the church ourselves.' It was almost like being another person in the room and watching this all happen. 'I agree,' said my wife. 'I've already rung a friend,' (the mother of the girl who had died) 'and she said there was a Sunday School at her church at the same time as the morning service, so I suggest we go there.' This in fact was the church at which the funeral of the young woman had been conducted. 'Okay,' I said, 'but if I don't like it we will go somewhere else next week.' And so we found ourselves that morning attending church together, for the first time since our marriage, and doing so as a family.

It was not, and still is not, a particularly fancy
building — in fact it is very plain and simple —
but then, as now, it was not the building I found
myself attracted to, but (and this is the most
difficult thing to put into words) it was the
sense of wholesomeness, warmth, love and understanding I felt as soon as I crossed the threshold
— a bit like coming home after a particularly
difficult day — and I hadn't yet met the people
properly! The service was plain and simple: no
reading from prayer books or cards. We sang a
hymn, the speaker read from the Bible, we sang
another hymn, he prayed ('Strange!' I thought.
He did not use fancy words, but seemed to speak
to God just as I had back there in the church
while on the dole), and then he spoke about the
passage of the Bible he had read. I don't remember now what he said. All I was conscious of
was a sense of wonder, peace and tenderness
such as I had never experienced in any other
service, anywhere.

We continued to attend the services and I
began to listen intently to the sermons. They
were a revelation to me. The Bible, hitherto a
book I only 'swore on', suddenly began to make
sense. At last questions I had asked over the
years were being answered. We were all made in
God's image, and at one time had had a relationship with our heavenly Creator, but things had
gone badly wrong in the beginning and, as a
result all the descendants of that first man, male
and female, were at odds with God. The disease
of sin — what the Bible called our wrong
thoughts, attitudes and way of life — now caused

a separation between God and us. This made sense of all the hate, jealousy, greed, violence, envy, adultery, lying and cheating that were common to all men everywhere, and suddenly I saw that this was my problem too; it was the reason I was like I was and, with all the desire in the world, I could never change my nature, any more than a leopard could change his spots. I did not have a personal relationship with God; what's more, I could never have one by my own efforts. As I read and studied the Bible, listened to the preaching of God's Word and read of other people's experiences in good Christian literature, it all began to make sense. Now I began to understand how it was possible to have a new and eternal relationship with this God, through faith in the finished work of Jesus Christ, whom God had sent into the world to pay the penalty for my sin; through repentance I could now have a new heart, that is, a new centre of being, and this by the supernatural action of God. I thought of these things for some six weeks from first attending the church, and one night realized that I needed to ask God to make me what I could never make myself — that is, a Christian, a follower of Jesus Christ, God's Son. So for perhaps the second time only in my life I really prayed, and asked God to forgive me, to make me a new person inside and help me to begin to serve him, instead of what I had done for thirty years, serving myself. I turned my back on my old life and began to follow the Lord Jesus Christ. Some weeks later my wife was also converted and so fourteen years ago we began a new life with God and with each other. Over these years we have learned many, many things about God — his love, faithfulness, care and provision for us day by day, year by year. We have learned, and indeed are still learning, what real love is, godly love for each other. God healed us individually first, then began to heal our relationship as man and wife, father and mother, and it is now our privilege to serve others in his church.

What difference does being a Christian make to my everyday living? I stress 'everyday' because Christianity is not just for Sundays.

I now know who I am — a child of God.

What am I doing here? Serving God my Maker by telling others about him, seeking to live a life pleasing to him.

Where am I going? This life is not all there is. Jesus, in the fourteenth chapter of John, told his disciples of a place where he was going and that he was going there to make a place for them, and that they would one day join him there.

God did not wait for me to be perfect, but he accepted me just as I was and then began to change me from the inside out, so that I no longer live for myself. I am no longer the centre of the universe; he is.

I seek to please him and be obedient to his plan for my life. This is hard sometimes for it means giving up what I want to do and doing what he wants. For instance, when people are rude, unkind, thoughtless, instead of giving up on them and having no more to do with them, Christ is teaching me to love them, just as he loves me with all my failings.

I have a new relationship with my wife, so that instead of my talking at her, we now talk together.

God is giving me a capacity to understand and to provide for the needs of others, so I now no longer see other people's problems as an intrusion into my life and am not as resentful when others make demands on my time, energy and love. I have a new relationship with my children, so that I am able to point them to one who can help, guide, keep and love them in all their circumstances.

I no longer have to pretend. We all wear masks — one for our neighbours, one for our friends, one for our family etc. — we are so scared they will see the real us and despise us, so we cover ourselves up with an image. Jesus Christ came to set us free, free to be ourselves, having forgiven all our past, present and future sins. Christians are able to look all men in the eye and not be afraid. Having said all that, I realize, with Paul the apostle, that I have not yet 'arrived'. I have still to learn a great deal more, yet I press on with God — towards the glorious future ahead when I will at last, face to face, see the one who died and gave himself for people like me and you.

Mike Wilde
February 1985

References

1. See, for example, Blaiklock, E.M., *The Acts of the Apostles,* IVP.
2. Bronowski, J., *The Ascent of Man,* B.B.C. Publications, p.68.
3. Hoyle, Fred, and Wickramasinghe, N.C., *Evolution from Space,* J.M. Dent & Sons.
4. Andersen, Francis, *Job,* (Tyndale Commentary), IVP, p.89.
5. Booker, Christopher, *The Seventies,* Allen Lane, p.292.
6. Bavinck, Herman, *Our Reasonable Faith,* Baker Book House, p.23.
7. Quoted by Chapman, Colin, *The Case for Christianity,* Lion Publications, p.231.
8. Milne, Bruce, *We Belong Together,* IVP, p.25.
9. Quoted in *The Case for Christianity,* p.26.
10. Forster, Roger, *Saturday Night ... Monday Morning,* IVP, p.63.
11. Casson, James, *Dying, The Greatest Adventure of My Life,* Christian Medical Fellowship, pp.18, 19, 34.
12. Cassette recording of Josif Ton speaking at Westminster Chapel, London, 1981.
13. Quoted in *The Case for Christianity,* p.64.
14. Pile, Stephen, *The Book of Heroic Failures,* Futura Publications, p.45.
15. Toffler, Alvin, *The Third Wave,* Pan Books, p.320.
16. Quoted by Chadwick, Owen, *The Reformation,* Penguin Books, p.45.
17. Sheikh, Bilquis, with Schneider, Richard, *I Dared to Call Him Father,* STL and Kingsway Publications.
18. Quoted by Hughes, Selwyn, *A Friend in Need,* Kingsway Publications.
19. Quoted by Atkinson, James, *The Great Light,* Paternoster, p.20.

*If after reading this book you would like
further help, please contact:*

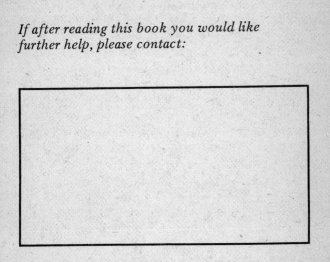

*Or write to the author, John Benton, who is the
pastor of Chertsey Street Baptist Church,
Guildford, Surrey, c/o the publishers:*

> *Evangelical Press,*
> *16-18 High Street,*
> *Welwyn,*
> *Hertfordshire,*
> *AL6 9EQ,*
> *England.*